MAY 2005

CHILDREN'S ROOM

BROCKTON PUBLIC LIBRARY

Uniquely
Rhode
Island

Katherine Moose

Heinemann Library
Chicago, Illinois

© 2004 Heinemann Library
a division of Reed Elsevier Inc.
Chicago, Illinois

Customer Service 888-454-2279

Visit our website at www.heinemannlibrary.com

All rights reserved. No part of this publication
may be reproduced or transmitted in any form or
by any means, electronic or mechanical, including
photocopying, recording, taping, or any
information storage and retrieval system, without
permission in writing from the publisher.

Designed by Heinemann Library
Printed in China by WKT Company Limited.

08 07 06 05 04
10 9 8 7 6 5 4 3 2 1

**Library of Congress
Cataloging-in-Publication Data**

Moose, Katherine.
    Uniquely Rhode Island/Katherine Moose.
      v. cm. -- (Heinemann state studies)
Includes bibliographical references and index.
Contents: Uniquely Rhode Island -- Rhode Island
climate -- Famous firsts -- Rhode Island state
symbols -- Rhode Island history and people --
The Cottages at Newport -- Rhode Island
government -- Rhode Island culture -- Rhode Island
folklore and legends -- Sports -- Rhode Island
businesses and products -- Attractions and
landmarks.
    ISBN 1-4034-4660-1 (lib. bdg.) --
ISBN 1-4034-4729-2
    1. Rhode Island -- Juvenile literature. [1. Rhode
Island.] I. Title.   II. Series.
  F79.3.M66 2004
  974.5'044 -- dc22
                                      2003027153

Cover Pictures

Top (left to right) Block Island Southeast
Lighthouse, Roger Williams, Rhode Island
state flag, yacht **Main** The Breakers

Acknowledgments
Development and photo research by
BOOK BUILDERS LLC

The author and publishers are grateful to the
following for permission to reproduce copyrighted
material:

Cover photographs by (top, L–R): Stock
Montage/Alamy; Joe Sohm/Alamy; Courtesy
Newport Convention & Visitors Bureau; (main):
Bob Krist/Corbis.

Title page (L–R): Michael Dwyer/Alamy; Everett
Johnson/Index Stock Imagery; Robert Harding
Picture Library LTD/Alamy. p. 5, 6, 7T, 9, 10, 14T,
14M, 15T, 25, 29, 41T, 43 Paul Pence; p. 7B Barry
Winiker/Index Stock Imagery; p. 8, 42, 45 IMA
for BOOK BUILDERS LLC; p. 11 Edward Stapel/AP
Photo; p. 12T Joe Sohm/Alamy; p. 12B One Mile
Up; p. 13T Beat Ernst; p. 13B Lynn Freeny/Alamy;
p. 15M Photo by SallyAnne Santos/Courtesy
Museum of Yachting, Newport, RI; p. 15B US
Mint; p. 16 Stock Montage/Alamy; p. 17 Library
of Congress; p. 19, 40 Eliot Cohen; p. 20
National Portrait Gallery, Smithsonian Institution,
Washington, DC/Art Resource NY; p. 22 SC
Photos/Alamy; p. 23 Ira Kearns/Photo courtesy
of the Preservation Society of Newport County;
p. 24T Robert Harding Picture Library LTD/Alamy;
p. 24B Bob Krist/Corbis; p. 26, 30 Michael
Dwyer/Alamy; p. 31 Everett Johnson/Index
Stock Imagery; p. 32 Envision; p. 34 R.
Capozzelli/Heinemann Library; p. 35 Courtesy of
Pawtucket Red Sox/Michael Gwynn; p. 36T Tom
Maguire; p. 36B Courtesy Newport Convention
& Visitors Bureau; p. 37 Lifespan/Robin Blossom;
p. 38 AP Photo; p. 39 Courtesy Vanguard
Sailboats/© Onne van der Wal.

Special thanks to Phoebe Simpson of the Rhode
Island Historical Society for her expert comments
in the preparation of this book.

Every effort has been made to contact copyright
holders of any material reproduced in this book.
Any omissions will be rectified in subsequent
printings if notice is given to the publisher.

Some words are shown in bold, **like this.**
You can find out what they mean by looking
in the glossary.

Contents

Uniquely Rhode Island

U*nique* means one of a kind. Rhode Island is unique in many ways. It is the smallest state in the United States, but has the longest name—"The State of Rhode Island and Providence Plantations." After the American **Revolutionary War** (1775–1783), when the American colonies became free from Great Britain, Rhode Island was the last state to sign the U.S. **Constitution.**

ORIGIN OF THE STATE'S NAME

One of the earliest **explorers** along the East Coast of what is now the United States was Adriaen Block from Holland. In 1614, he sighted what is today Rhode Island. Block thought the red clay beaches were very unusual because most beaches are sandy or rocky. He named it "Roodt Eylandt," which means "Red Island" in Dutch.

In 1663, Rhode Island received its present name when it received a **charter** from King Charles II of England, making it an English colony. At that time, Aquidneck Island was known as the Isle of Rhodes, or Rhode Island. The island, located in Narragansett Bay, is now the site of Newport and Portsmouth. Providence, the first city settled in Rhode Island by English colonists, was then called Providence Plantations. The name of the colony combined the two names—Rhode Island and Providence Plantations.

THE SMALLEST STATE

Rhode Island, located in the northeastern United States, is the smallest of the 50 states with an area of only 1,214 square miles. North to south, the state measures 48 miles, and east to west, it is 37 miles.

MAJOR CITIES

Providence, the largest city and state capital, is one of the three largest cities in New England. Located at the northern end of Narragansett Bay, the city has a population of about 175,000 and is a major port.

One of the most unusual events in the city is Water Fire. Several evenings during the year a series of 100 bonfires burn just above the rivers that pass through the middle of downtown Providence. The fires light up downtown and the parks. People wander along the rivers and listen to music. The fires are lit from sunset until after midnight by performers dressed in black who float by in boats. People come from all over the world to see this display.

Warwick is the second-largest city with a population of 85,000 people. The oldest part of Warwick, Pawtuxet Village, was settled in 1642. Pawtuxet means "Little Falls" in the Narragansett language. Located southwest of Providence on the Narragansett Bay, Warwick has 39 miles of coastline and a rich nautical history.

The area surrounding this fishing shed on Apponaug Cove dates from the 1600s. Warwick's town hall also can be seen in the background.

Cranston, the third-largest city with a population of 79,000 people, was originally part of Providence. It separated from Providence in 1754 and became a town. Providence, Warwick, and Cranston were once **textile** manufacturing towns. Today, the area is known as the jewelry capital of the world. Jewelry companies located there include Trifari, Monet, Swarovski, and A.T. Cross, which also manufactures pens.

Rhode Island's Geography and Climate

Rhode Island's location in New England along the Atlantic coast influences the state's geography and climate.

LAND

Rhode Island is divided into two geographic regions— the Coastal Lowlands and the New England Upland. The Coastal Lowlands make up about half of the state. This area includes the mainland and the islands along Narragansett Bay and the Atlantic Ocean. To the east lie salt ponds, beaches, and rocky shores. Salt ponds are shallow pools located farther inland from the beaches.

The rolling hills in the Eastern New England Upland include the highest point in Rhode Island. Jerimoth Hill is 812 feet above sea level.

The Eastern New England Upland covers the northwestern part of the state. This area has rolling hills, trees, small ponds, and lakes.

Narragansett Bay

The Narragansett Bay is the major waterway of Rhode Island. It is used for shipping, fishing, and recreational boating. Because of pollution, however, the bay has sometimes been closed to shell fishing and swimming. For many years, people have been trying to protect the bay from pollution and overdevelopment. The *Save The Bay Foundation* leads this **conservation** effort by watching over activities that could lead to pollution and taking the lead in actions that help to keep the bay clean.

CLIMATE

Rhode Island has a temperate climate because of the influence of the Gulf Stream. The Gulf Stream is an area of warm water in the Atlantic Ocean that moves northward from Florida along the Eastern Coast. Unusual trees and plants,

*Green Animals is one of the oldest **topiary** gardens in the United States. Located in Portsmouth, it has more than 80 topiary in the shape of animals and other figures.*

Average Annual Precipitation
Rhode Island

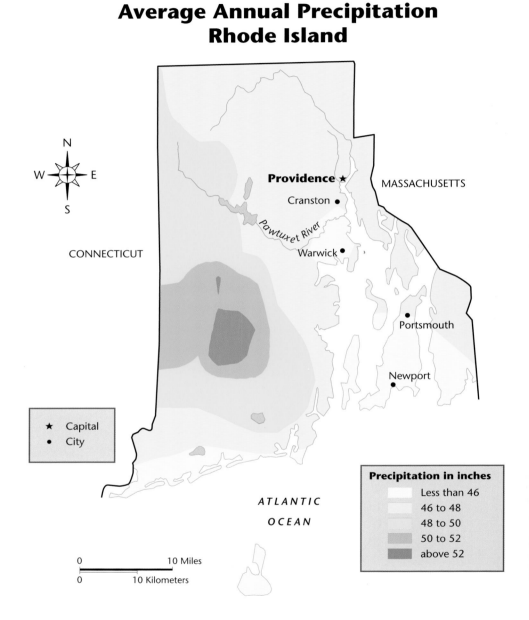

N

W—E

S

CONNECTICUT

Providence ★

MASSACHUSETTS

Cranston ●

Pawtuxet River

Warwick ●

Portsmouth ●

Newport ●

★ Capital
● City

ATLANTIC

OCEAN

Precipitation in inches

Less than 46
46 to 48
48 to 50
50 to 52
above 52

0   10 Miles

0   10 Kilometers

including the weeping beech and the Japanese hem-
lock, grow in Rhode Island because of its temperate climate. The average temperature in January is 20°F and
in July is 81°F. Rhode Island's average annual precipitation—rain and snow—is 45 inches.

Famous Firsts

RELIGIOUS FIRSTS

Roger Williams founded the first **Baptist** Church in America in 1638. Williams came to the Massachusetts colony from England in 1631 to escape religious **persecution.** He believed in religious **toleration** and the **separation of church and state.** The strict Puritan religious leaders who controlled the Massachusetts forced Williams from the colony. He fled into the wilderness and established a small settlement, which he named Providence. Williams's colony became a refuge for people seeking religious freedom, including Baptists, **Quakers,** and Jews.

Quakers first came to Newport in 1657. They established the first **Friends Meetinghouse** in the colonies in 1699.

Beginning in 1658, many Jews began to settle in Newport. They built Touro **Synagogue** in 1762. It is the oldest synagogue in North America and holds the oldest **Torah** in the United States.

Touro Synagogue was designed by Peter Harrison, a famous New England architect. The synagogue is named for Isaac de Touro who arrived in Newport in 1758 from Amsterdam, The Netherlands.

HISTORIC FIRSTS

The gravesite of Elizabeth Alden Pabodie, the first English child born in New England, is located in Little Compton. Born in 1624, she was the daughter of John and Priscilla Alden who had sailed from Europe to Plymouth, Massachusetts, on the *Mayflower* in 1620. Elizabeth Alden married William Pabodie in 1644 and later moved to Rhode Island. She died in 1717.

Rhode Island was the first colony to ban **slavery** on May 18, 1652. This was more than 200 years before Congress abolished slavery after the **Civil War** (1861–1865). However, the law was mostly ignored and slavery continued.

In the 1600s, the White Horse Tavern served as the meeting place for the colony's General Assembly and Criminal Courts.

Nine Men's Misery Monument in Cumberland is the oldest known monument to **veterans** in the United States. The monument, erected in 1928, commemorates the nine men killed by Native Americans in 1676.

The White Horse Tavern in Newport is the oldest inn still operating in the United States. It dates from 1673. The third owner, William Mayes, was a notorious pirate.

The first U.S. traffic law was created in 1678 when authorities banned galloping horses on the streets of Newport.

In 1749, Abraham Redwood founded the Redwood Library and **Atheneum** in Newport, making it the oldest library in the United States. Many books from its original 750 titles disappeared during the **Revolutionary War** (1775–1783), when the British soldiers moved into the library.

The oldest **carousel** in the United States still in use is the Flying Horse Carousel in Watch Hill. The carousel was made around 1876 by Charles Dare. The horses are carved from a single piece of wood and have real tails and manes, leather saddles, and **agate** eyes.

In 2000 Ruth J. Simmons became president of Brown University in Providence. She is the first African American woman to head an **Ivy League** university.

Ruth J. Simmons is also the first female president of Brown University.

Sports Firsts

Rhode Island has many firsts in sports. Polo was played for the first time in the United States in 1876 in Portsmouth. In Newport, the first open golf tournament was played in 1895 and the first National Lawn Tennis Championship was held in 1899. Brown University's football team, the "Iron Men," played in the first Rose Bowl game in 1915.

Rhode Island's State Symbols

Rhode Island's state flag is flown over government and public buildings throughout the state.

The state seal is used by the government on state documents.

RHODE ISLAND STATE FLAG

The state flag was officially adopted in 1897. A golden anchor is centered on a white background. Beneath the anchor is a blue ribbon with the motto "Hope" in gold letters. A circle of thirteen stars represents the thirteen original colonies.

RHODE ISLAND STATE SEAL

The state seal was adopted in 1897. The outer circle of the seal reads "Seal of the State of Rhode Island and Providence Plantations 1636".

STATE MOTTO: HOPE

Rhode Island's motto was adopted in 1875. It appears on the state flag and the state seal.

STATE NICKNAME: OCEAN STATE

Rhode Island's official nickname "Ocean State" is used to promote recreation and tourism along its coasts. Other nicknames are "Little Rhody," "Smallest State," and "Plantation State."

STATE SONG: "RHODE ISLAND'S IT FOR ME"

"Rhode Island's It for Me" became the Rhode Island state song in 1946. Charlie Hall wrote the words and Maria Day composed the music.

"Rhode Island's It for Me"

I've been to every state we have,
and I think I'm inclined to say
that Rhody stole my heart:
You can keep the forty-nine.

Herring gulls that dot the sky,
blue waves that paint the rocks,
waters rich with Neptune's life,
the boats that line the docks.

I see the lighthouse flickering
to help the sailors see.
There's a place for everyone:
Rhode Island's it for me.

Rhode Island, oh, Rhode Island
surrounded by the sea.
Some people roam the earth for home;
Rhode Island's it for me.

STATE FLOWER: VIOLET

Schoolchildren in Rhode Island voted the violet as the state flower on Arbor Day in 1897. But it was not until March 11, 1968, that the flower was officially adopted as the state flower. Rhode Island was the last state to adopt a state flower.

Violets are a common purple flower found in the eastern United States. They bloom in late April or early May.

STATE TREE: RED MAPLE

The red maple became the state tree in 1964. The red maple is also known as scarlet maple, swamp maple, soft maple, Carolina red maple, Drummond red maple, and water maple. It is one of the most common trees in the state.

The red maple has crimson flowers in the spring before the leaves appear.

The Rhode Island Red was developed in Rhode Island in the mid-1800s.

STATE BIRD: RHODE ISLAND RED

The Rhode Island Red is an American breed of chicken that has reddish legs and feathers. It became the state bird in 1954. The Rhode Island Red has helped make **poultry** a major industry in the United States. The chickens are known for high-quality brown eggs.

The quahog is a hard-shelled clam.

STATE SHELL: QUAHOG

The word *quahog* comes from the Narragansett name "poquauhock". The quahog's scientific name is a Latin word meaning "wages." The Native Americans used quahog shells to make beads that they used as money. It was adopted as Rhode Island's official state shell on July 1, 1987.

STATE ROCK: CUMBERLANDITE

Cumberlandite, a dark brown or black rock with white markings, became the state rock in 1966. Cumberlandite is about 1.5 billion years old and was formed when a small volcano erupted, mixing 24 different minerals together with molten rock. When it cooled, it formed a slightly magnetic rock. Cumberlandite has never been found outside Rhode Island.

The location of the only known deposit is a 3.7 acre site in Cumberland called the Iron Mine Hill.

STATE MINERAL: BOWENITE

Bowenite became the state mineral in 1966. The stone is related to jade and is found in several different colors. It is a semiprecious stone and is often used in jewelry. Bowenite is found in the northern part of the state along with limestone.

Because of its appearance and magnetism, Cumberlandite is often mistaken for a meteorite.

STATE YACHT: *COURAGEOUS*

The sailboat *Courageous* competed in five **America's Cup** races, more races than any other yacht. In 1997, it was donated to the Museum of Yachting in Newport. *Courageous* was designated as Rhode Island's State Yacht on July 13, 2000.

RHODE ISLAND STATE QUARTER

The reverse of the Rhode Island quarter shows an antique sailboat sailing on Narragansett Bay with the Pell Bridge in the background. The bridge is named for former Rhode Island Senator Claiborne Pell.

The Rhode Island quarter, dated 2001, is the thirteenth of the state commemorative series.

Courageous is 66-1/2 feet long, weighs 57,000 pounds, and has a sail area of 1,770 square feet.

Rhode Island's History and People

The story of Rhode Island begins in prehistory—the time before events were written down. The earliest people were nomads who followed the animals they hunted for food and clothing.

NATIVE AMERICANS

In the early 1600s, European explorers found several Native American tribes living in what is today Rhode Island. The largest tribe was the Narragansett. The Wampanoags lived along the eastern shore of Narragansett Bay. The Nipmucks, a small tribe, lived the northwestern corner of today's Rhode Island. **Anthropologists** estimate that about 7,000 Native Americans lived in the area when the Europeans arrived.

Roger Williams strongly believed in rights for Native Americans.

EUROPEAN SETTLEMENT

Roger Williams, a teacher and minister, founded Rhode Island after coming to the Massachusetts Bay colony from England in 1631. In 1636, he was exiled from Massachusetts for his religious beliefs, which included **separation of church and state.**

Anne Hutchinson

Anne Hutchinson and her husband William, a cloth merchant, moved to Massachusetts in 1634. In 1638, the Hutchinsons, John Coggeshall, and William Coddington left Massachusetts because of their religious beliefs. They purchased Aquidneck Island from the Narragansett and founded Portsmouth in 1638. Anne Hutchinson was the first woman in the Americas to found a town.

He founded his settlement on land purchased from the Narragansett and named it Providence, in gratitude for "God's merciful providence to me in my distress."

Other leaders who wanted freedom of worship soon established communities near Narragansett Bay. These communities joined together, and in 1663, King Charles II of England granted them a **royal charter.** This document allowed them self-government and freedom of religion.

SHIPPING AND TRADE

By the mid-1700s, Rhode Island's merchants traded with the other colonies along the eastern coast of the North America, Great Britain, and other parts of the world. Bristol and Warren became important ports.

Ships participated in what was known as the Triangle Trade. Molasses was brought from the West Indies to make rum in Rhode Island. The rum was traded for **slaves** in Africa who were, in turn, brought to the colonies to be sold. Trade made a number of Rhode Islanders very wealthy.

THE AMERICAN REVOLUTION

As trade became more important, Great Britain began to tax the products brought into the colonies and make new laws. Rhode Islanders believed these new laws hurt its trade. For example, the Sugar Act of 1764 imposed strict limits on the molasses trade, which in turn hurt the Triangle Trade.

As tensions between Britain and the colonies increased, the Rhode Island colonists were the first to openly rebel. In 1772, the *Gaspee,* a British ship went aground in Narragansett Bay. The colonists set fire to the ship and let it sink. Later, in October 1775, the first British troops sent to stop the **Revolutionary War** (1775–1783) landed in Newport. They occupied the city until 1779.

On October 13, 1775, the **Continental Congress** in Philadelphia passed a **resolution** to create the United States Navy. Ezek Hopkins, of Providence, was the first commander of the colonial navy and the first ship, the *Katy,* was built in Providence. In the first naval battle of the Revolutionary War, the *Katy* captured the British ship *Diana,* which had been blockading American ports. The *Katy* was later renamed Providence and commanded by John Paul Jones, the "Father of the American Navy". On May 4, 1776, Rhode Island was the first colony to declare **independence** from Great Britain.

The Battle of Rhode Island

The Battle of Rhode Island was the first time an all African American regiment—the Rhode Island First Regiment—fought for the United States. In August 29, 1778, the Rhode Island First fought the British near Portsmouth, trying to force the British from Newport. The battle ended with the British still in control of Newport. However, they left the port city the following year.

On May 29, 1790, Rhode Island was the last of the thirteen colonies to **ratify** the United States Constitution and become a state. Many Rhode Islanders were afraid that the new **federal government** would become too strong. Rhode Island Quakers, in particular, opposed the new Constitution because it did not ban **slavery.**

THE INDUSTRIAL REVOLUTION

Until the late 1700s, the main industries in Rhode Island were boat building, farming, and trade. Everything was made by hand. In 1790, Moses Brown and Samuel Slater built a cotton mill at the Pawtucket Falls on the Blackstone River. For the first time, cotton yarn was spun by waterpower. With the launch of this new revolution—the Industrial Revolution—products could be mass-produced by power-driven machines. The rise of industry played a big part in the growth of Rhode Island's economy.

Slater's Mill, 1790

In 1789, Great Britain was the only country in the world using water-powered machines to make cloth. The British would not let anyone make copies of the plans to build the machines. But Samuel Slater memorized the plans. With financial help from Moses Brown, a Providence business leader, Slater built mills in Pawtucket in 1790. Other mills around New England soon followed, thus creating a thriving textile industry.

FAMOUS PEOPLE

Robert Gray (1755–1806), merchant sailor. Born in Tiverton, Gray worked for a Massachusetts trading company after the Revolutionary War (1775–1783) that sent him by ship to Oregon. He then went to China to sell the sea otter pelts he had bought in Oregon in exchange for silk and spices. On leaving, he sailed west from China to Boston. This made him the first American merchant sailor to **circumnavigate** the globe.

Clement Clarke Moore (1779–1863), author and professor. Moore lived in Newport and wrote the famous poem "The Night before Christmas" for his children in 1822. The original title of the poem was "A Visit from St. Nicholas."

Julia Ward Howe was an important social reformer. She worked to end slavery and helped women and the handicapped gain rights.

Matthew C. Perry (1794–1858), naval hero. Born in South Kingstown, Perry supervised the construction of the first naval steamship, *The Fulton,* and in 1837 became its commanding officer. In 1853, he commanded four American ships that sailed to Tokyo, Japan. Until that time Japan had not allowed any foreigners in the country. In 1854, a treaty was signed that allowed American ships to enter into Japanese ports.

Julia Ward Howe (1819–1910), writer. Howe, who lived in Newport and Portsmouth, was opposed to slavery. She composed the words to the song the "Battle Hymn of the Republic." She also believed in rights for women, including voting, and introduced the idea of establishing a Mother's Day in the United States.

Stephen Wilcox (1830–1893) and **George Babcock** (1832–1893), inventors. Wilcox and Babcock lived in Westerly, but moved to Brooklyn, New York, where they invented the water tube steam boiler to run electric generators. They established the Babcock & Wilcox Company, which makes boilers to power U.S. Navy and Merchant Marine ships that are still used today.

Napoleon "Larry" Lajoie (1874–1959), baseball player. Lajoie, born in Woonsocket, was the first batting champion in the American League. He batted .422 in 1901 for the Philadelphia Athletics, an unbroken American League record. On May 23, 1901, he became the first major league player to be intentionally walked with the bases loaded. He was inducted into the Baseball Hall of Fame in 1937.

George M. Cohan (1878–1942), actor and composer. Cohan, born in Providence, starred from an early age in dance and song acts. He wrote more than 500 songs, including **patriotic** songs such as "I'm a Yankee Doodle Dandy" (1904), "You're a Grand Old Flag" (1906), and "Over There" (1917). George Cohan received a medal from the U.S. Congress for his patriotism.

The United States honored George M. Cohan with a postage stamp.

John Pastore (1907–2000), former governor of Rhode Island and Senator. Pastore, born in Providence, was elected governor of Rhode Island twice, first in 1946 and later in 1948. He became the first person of Italian descent to be elected to the U.S. Senate in 1950.

Felix de Weldon (1907–2003), sculptor. De Weldon was one of the most famous artists of the 1900s. His Marine

President Dwight D. Eisenhower dedicated the Marine Corps War Memorial on November 10, 1954.

Corps War Memorial of servicemen raising the flag on the island of Iwo Jima during **World War II** is next to Arlington National Cemetery near Washington, D.C.

Irving R. Levine (1922–), newscaster. Born in Pawtucket, Levine was a news reporter for NBC for more than 40 years, longer than any other correspondent. He was the first to cover business full time. His scripts and other materials are now at the "Irving R. Levine Collection" at the Library of Congress in Washington, D.C.

Leonard Woodcock (1911–), union leader. Born in Providence, Woodcock became president of the United Auto Workers (UAW) association in 1970. He worked to help workers receive good wages, pensions, and have a safe workplace. He also opposed job **discrimination.**

Chris Van Allsburg (1949–), author, sculptor, illustrator. Van Allsburg moved to Providence in 1972. His children's books include *The Garden of Abdul Gasazi, Jumanji, The Polar Express,* and *Zathura.*

David Macaulay (1946–), author. Macaulay moved to Rhode Island when he was sixteen years old. He loved to draw and graduated from the Rhode Island School of Design, where he still teaches. He won the Caldecott Medal for his book, *Black and White,* and is the author of many other children's books including *Castle* and *The Way Things Work.*

The Cottages at Newport

After the **Civil War** (1861–1865), many wealthy families from New York and other cities began building magnificent summer houses, which they called "cottages," in Newport. The houses they built often had more than 40 rooms, including a ballroom, plus servants' quarters. The houses featured formal gardens and large lawns that stretched to the Atlantic Ocean or to Narragansett Bay.

These wealthy people came to Newport because the weather was much cooler during the summer. They usually stayed only three or four months.

Kingscote's dining room, added in 1881, includes Tiffany glass around the fireplace and the large bay window.

Kingscote was the first of the cottages built along Bellevue Avenue. George Noble Jones, a plantation owner from Savannah, Georgia, built the **Gothic Revival** style house between 1839 and 1841. Later, in 1864, the mansion was sold to William H. King, a China trade merchant, who named it Kingscote.

THE GILDED AGE

Because fortunes were spent on luxuries during the late 1880s, this era is often called the Gilded Age. Gilded means covered with gold. At the time, the richest person in the United States was Cornelius Vanderbilt (1794–1877), who made his fortune in the steamship and

Designed by Richard Morris Hunt, a famous American architect, Marble House includes more than 500,000 cubic feet of marble.

railroad industries. When he died, he left almost $95 million to his son, William. His grandson, also named William, built Marble House, which is modeled after a French castle. The mansion, completed in 1892, took almost 4 years to build and cost more than $11 million.

The Breakers, an Italian **Renaissance** style house, was built by Cornelius Vanderbilt II, also a grandson of Commodore Vanderbilt, in 1895. Also designed by Richard Morris Hunt, it is Newport's grandest cottage. The Breakers has 70 rooms and overlooks the Atlantic Ocean.

The iron entrance gates are 30 feet high and include the wrought-iron initials CV for Cornelius Vanderbilt.

Estate Preservation

Because thousands of visitors come each year to see the cottages at Newport, these houses must be repaired and maintained continuously. In 2002, the Breakers was **renovated** at a cost of $2 million. Work included rebuilding several chimneys, replacing more than 30,000 roof tiles, and restoring or replacing the rooftop skylights. The outside walls were power washed, the windows painted, and cracks repaired.

Rhode Island's State Government

Rhode Island's government is based in Providence, the capital. Similar to the **federal government** in Washington, D.C., Rhode Island's government is made up of three branches—the legislative, the executive, and the judicial branches.

The government is based on the state **constitution** adopted in 1842. Before that date, a **royal charter,** issued in 1663 by England's King Charles II, served as the state's constitution.

Providence became the sole capital of Rhode Island in 1900. Newport had been the joint capital until then.

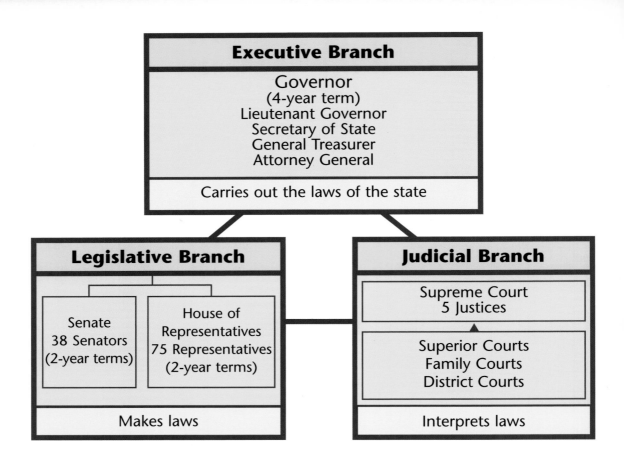

Executive Branch

Governor
(4-year term)
Lieutenant Governor
Secretary of State
General Treasurer
Attorney General

Carries out the laws of the state

Legislative Branch

Senate
38 Senators
(2-year terms)

House of
Representatives
75 Representatives
(2-year terms)

Makes laws

Judicial Branch

Supreme Court
5 Justices

Superior Courts
Family Courts
District Courts

Interprets laws

LEGISLATIVE BRANCH

Rhode Island's **legislature,** called the General Assembly, makes the state's laws. It consists of two houses—the senate and the house of representatives. In 2004, the senate included 38 members and the house was made up of 75 representatives. All legislators are elected to two-year terms and are not restricted by term limits.

A bill, or proposed law, may start in either house of the General Assembly. After a bill has been approved by a majority, or more than half, of the members of both houses, it is sent to the governor. If the governor signs the bill, it becomes a law. If the governor vetoes, or rejects, the bill, it becomes law only if a three-fifths majority of the legislature votes to override the veto.

The Rhode Island state capitol was built between 1895 and 1903.

EXECUTIVE BRANCH

The executive branch enforces the state's laws and runs the state from day to day. The governor is the head of this branch. The lieutenant governor is the second-highest state official. Voters elect these two government leaders to a four-year term of office. The governor is limited to two four-year terms.

Voters also elect three other officials in the executive branch to four-year terms. The secretary of state supervises elections and helps register voters. The general treasurer collects the state's tax money. The attorney general serves as the state's legal adviser.

JUDICIAL BRANCH

The judicial branch of the government interprets Rhode Island's laws. The court system is made up of district courts, family courts, superior courts, and the supreme court.

The district courts hear cases involving small claims—under $5,000—as well as violations of city regulations and certain **misdemeanors,** usually when a jury is not involved. Thirteen judges serve on the state's district courts. They are appointed by the governor and confirmed by the senate.

The family court helps resolve problems involving children and families. These cases involve divorce, child custody, and child support. Rhode Island's family court is made up of twelve justices, who are appointed by the governor and then confirmed by the senate. **Appeals** from family court decisions go directly to the supreme court.

The superior court is the trial court of jurisdiction over **felony cases** and **civil cases** of more than $10,000. The superior court also handles personal injury and property damage suits. The twenty judges who serve the superior court's four districts are appointed by the governor and confirmed by the state senate. Appeals from the superior court are heard by the supreme court.

The supreme court is the highest court in the state. The supreme court consists of a chief justice and four associate justices, who are appointed by the governor and then confirmed by both the senate and the house of representatives. As the court of last resort, the supreme court hears appeals cases from the lower courts.

Rhode Island's Culture

Culture in Rhode Island is a blend of its history, nautical past, natural beauty, and diverse population.

The Black Ships Festival, which began in 1983, commemorates the historic achievements of Commodore Matthew C. Perry of Newport and the signing of the Treaty of Kanagawa. Black Ships refers to the Japanese term for foreign ships, which were excluded from Japan until 1854. In that year, Commodore Perry negotiated the Treaty of Kanagawa, the first treaty between the United States and Japan, which brought the two countries together as trading partners.

The Black Ships Festival is celebrated in Newport and its Japanese Sister City, Shimoda, each July.

THE CONVERGENCE INTERNATIONAL ARTS FESTIVAL

For three weeks in September each year, Providence comes alive as artists and sculptors from across the country gather for the Convergence International Arts Festival. Since its founding in 1988, the festival has become one of the best-known arts festivals in the nation. The festival is centered in downtown

The most famous jazz musicians in the world have played at the Newport Jazz Festival, including Louis Armstrong, Ella Fitzgerald, Miles Davis, and Billie Holiday.

Providence, but other Rhode Island towns also take part in the fun. Today, the festival highlights art, sculpture, short films and videos, as well as the performing arts, such as dance. Visitors can view the works of art, enjoy music, and eat local treats.

THE NEWPORT JAZZ FESTIVAL

Founded in 1954 by George Wein and a few of Newport's residents, the Newport Jazz Festival has become famous around the world. Jazz musicians come to Newport every summer to play all types of jazz music and entertain visitors. The festival takes place at Fort Adams State Park—right on the water. In addition to lawn seats, jazz fans can enjoy the music as they float in their motorboats, yachts, and rubber **dinghies.**

THE NEWPORT FOLK FESTIVAL

George Wein, founder of the Newport Jazz Festival, started the Newport Folk Festival in 1959. The folk festival quickly became popular as folk music fans filled the Fort Adams State Park. Famous musicians, including James Taylor, Joni Mitchell, Joan Baez, Janis Joplin, and Peter, Paul & Mary have performed at the festival. Later, the festival began to highlight other types of music, such as the bluegrass music of Bill Monroe and the blues of Muddy Waters. Today, fans come from all over the world to hear their favorite artists.

Rhode Island's Food

Many of the dishes made in Rhode Island date back to the cooking of the early Native Americans or were brought to the state by **immigrants.**

BOUNTY FROM THE SEA

Among the many creatures that live on the Rhode Island coast, some of the most common and tasty are clams. Whether they are steamed or eaten raw on the half-shell, cooked in chowder or deep-fried in a sandwich, clams have long been a food source in Rhode Island. Clams were once considered so valuable that area Native Americans used *quahogs,* a type of clam, as money. Called *wampum,* these clams gained their value from the time and effort it took to drill a lengthwise hole in their cylindrical shape.

RHODE ISLAND SHORE DINNER

Shore dinners, sometimes called a clambake, are a traditional pastime of the summer. The basic ingredients for a shore dinner are chowder, clam cakes, lobster, clams (known as steamers), corn on the cob, and potatoes.

A shore dinner can be served in a restaurant or cooked on the beach.

Rhode Island Johnnycakes

Johnnycakes are a Rhode Island version of pancakes. But these pancakes are made from white cornmeal, not flour. The name may come from "journey cake," because people once took them, already cooked, on their travels. Some people, however, think the name comes from *joniken,* a native word for corn.

Be sure you have an adult help you when you make these.

2 cups white cornmeal	1/2 cup milk
1 stick butter, softened	butter (for frying)
1 teaspoon salt	Maple syrup, butter, or honey (for topping)
2 cups boiling water	

Combine the cornmeal, salt, and butter in a large mixing bowl. Pour in the boiling water, constantly stirring with a spoon. Then add the milk. Beat until the mixture is thickened. Melt butter in a heated skillet. Using a measuring cup, pour 1/4 cup of the mixture into the skillet to form a pancake. Fry each johnnycake for about three minutes, or until the edges brown. Keep them warm in the oven. Serve with butter and maple syrup or honey. Makes 8 round cakes.

IMMIGRANT DISHES

As people from Europe and other parts of the world moved to Rhode Island, they brought their favorite dishes with them. Many Portuguese people settled in Rhode Island, and continued their traditional job as fishers. One Portuguese dish that is found throughout Rhode Island is kale soup, a hearty broth of spicy Portuguese sausage, kale, beans, potatoes, and other vegetables.

Rhode Island's Folklore and Legends

Legends and folklore are stories that are not totally true, but are often based on bits of truth. These stories help people understand things that cannot be easily explained. They also teach lessons to younger generations. All peoples tell these types of stories.

THE *PALATINE*

In late 1750, a ship left Great Britain bound for the American colonies. The *Palatine* left port with a full crew, a long list of passengers, and a hull full of goods. Fierce Atlantic storms tossed the tiny ship and blew it off course. The crew became afraid, killed the ship's captain, and took the passengers prisoner. One morning, the passengers awoke and discovered that the crew had stolen all of their money and food and had abandoned the ship. Terrified, they could do nothing but ride out the storms and hope the ship would soon reach land.

The ruined *Palatine* came to rest off the coast of Block Island. The people living on the island bravely rescued the starving passengers from the wreck and then set fire to the ship so that it would not endanger any passing ships. According to legend, every year on the anniversary of the tragedy, the wrecked *Palatine* reappears off the shore and burns.

THE WAMPANOAGS' VISITORS

The Wampanoag are known as The People of the First Light, because of their geographical location near the eastern coast of Narragansett Bay. The Wampanoag people have lived in the area for many thousands of years. Once, the Wampanoag nation included more than 12,000 warriors and their lands covered northern and eastern Rhode Island, most of Massachusetts, and reached west to New York. The Wampanoag believe the ancient Phoenicians—from the eastern shore of the Mediterranean Sea—were the first to visit their lands. Other peoples followed, including the Vikings, the Irish, and the Italians. The Wampanoag greeted them all in peace. Did all these people reach what is today New England before the Pilgrims?

THE KING OF EXETER

Around 1790, James Lillibridge of Exeter arrived in Tranquebar on the east coast of India. There he met Prince Holkar, the rajah, or king, of Indore. After Mr. Lil-

libridge had been in India for fifteen years, he went to found his own kingdom. Before long, his kingdom was larger than the prince's and he had a 7,000-soldier army. However, he got homesick and wanted to return to Rhode Island. Before he left, he held a large dinner. He decided to jump his horse over the banquet table. As he galloped across the room, the horse's hoofs became entangled in the rug. The horse fell with King James underneath and he died on September 23, 1806. He never returned to Rhode Island.

Rhode Island's Sports Teams

Rhode Island has several good college teams and one minor league baseball team.

MINOR LEAGUE BASEBALL

The Pawtucket PawSox, the Boston Red Sox's Triple A team, play at McCoy Stadium in Pawtucket. The team has produced a number of great players for the Boston Red Sox, including Wade Boggs, who had more than 3,000 career hits; Roger Clemens, who was a 5-time Cy Young Award winner, and later pitched for the New York Yankees; and Nomar Garciaparra, one of baseball's best shortstops. In 1981, the PawSox and Rochester Red Wings met in the longest professional baseball game ever played. Play began on April 18th and was finally over 33 innings later, on June 23rd. The PawSox won 3–2.

On August 10, 2003, Bronson Arroyo pitched the fourth nine-inning perfect game in the 120-year history of the International League when the PawSox beat the Buffalo Bisons, 7–0.

COLLEGE TEAMS

The University of Rhode Island's sports teams are called the Rams. The teams are part of the Atlantic 10 Conference and NCAA Division I. The University, located in

Billy Donovan was named the Southeast Regional MVP in 1987, when he led the Providence Friars to the Final Four.

Kingston, opened the Rhode Island Athletic Hall of Fame in 1959. Former University of Rhode Island pitcher Jared Trout was named the Oakland Athletics "Best Late-Round Draft Pick" by the magazine *Baseball America.* Trout helped lead the Rams to the Atlantic 10 East Division title in 2003 before being selected in the 28th round by the Athletics.

Providence College has produced a number of top athletes in basketball and track. The teams are called the Friars. In 1987, Coach Rick Pitino and his star guard, Billy Donovan, led the Friars to the Final Four in basketball. In 2003, six former Friars, including Pitino, were inducted into the New England Basketball Hall of Fame. Donovan now coaches the University of Florida's basketball team.

The boats used for many years in the America's Cup Race were called 12-meter boats. They are 69 feet long and have very tall masts.

BOATING AND SAILING

The oldest yachting race in the United States is the **America's Cup** Race. The first race occurred in England in 1851 when *America* beat sixteen English boats and won the "One Hundred Guinea Cup." The race was moved to Newport in 1930 and renamed the America's Cup. In 1983, the United States lost the America's Cup when the American yacht *Liberty* lost to *Australia II.* The United States had held the Cup for 132 years—the longest winning streak in U.S. sports history.

Rhode Island's Businesses and Products

Rhode Island has been a manufacturing center for toys, textiles, rubber goods, printing, boat building, metals, machinery, and jewelry for more than 200 years. More recently, the health services industry became the largest employer in the state, bringing about 33,000 jobs to the state.

HEALTH SERVICES

Rhode Island's largest industry had its beginnings when Butler Hospital opened in 1847 and was followed by the Providence Reform School for wayward children in 1850. Butler Hospital still serves the Rhode Island community. **Pharmaceutical** and biotechnology companies, medical instrument firms, health-insurance companies, nursing homes, and medical research institutions are all involved in health services.

Rhode Island Hospital is a private, 719-bed hospital and academic medical center. Founded in 1863, the hospital is the largest of the state's hospitals. The hospital is a leading heart-care and cancer-care center, and provides special services to children at its Hasbro Children's Hospital.

Rhode Island Hospital is the largest employer in the state with 5,800 employees.

The Hasbro Corporation makes many toys, including Mr. Potato Head.

HASBRO

The largest toy company in the world is located in Pawtucket. Henry and Helal Hassenfeld founded Hasbro in 1923 and first sold cloth and fabric. Later, the company began to manufacture pencil boxes and school supplies. The company branched out and bought smaller companies that made toys, such as Playskool, Tonka Toys, Mr. Potato Head, Play-Doh, Candyland, and Easy-Bake Oven. In 1991, Hasbro bought Parker Brothers, which made the game, Monopoly.

BOAT BUILDING

Boat building is the oldest industry in Rhode Island. Today, about 35 companies produce boats that are 20 to 90 or more feet long. The companies, mostly located in

Gorham Manufacturing Company

Jabez Gorham (1792–1869), a silversmith and jeweler, was the first to make "French **filigree**" jewelry and a special kind of gold chain known as the Gorham chain. In 1831, he founded the Gorham Manufacturing Company to make silver spoons. Later, the company manufactured statues and memorials. Gorham created the monument of George Washington in the U.S. Capitol Rotunda in Washington, D.C., as well as the statue of President Theodore Roosevelt outside the Museum of Natural History in New York. Gorham created "The Independent Man" on top of the State House in Providence in 1899.

the towns of Bristol, Middletown, Portsmouth, and Warren, employ between 900 and 1,200 workers. About 60 percent of the workers make sailboats, while the others make powerboats. The largest employer is TPI Composites in Warren, a manufacturer of 22- to 60-foot fiberglass sailing yachts. Other large employers include Ted Hood Enterprises, Blount Industries, Carroll Marine, Eric Goetz Custom Sailboats, and Sunfish Laser.

Equipment for boats such as sails, oars, and winches are also manufactured in Rhode Island. One of the oldest yacht yards is Herreshoff in Bristol, which built several America's Cup boats. The first **torpedo boat,** *Stiletto,* was built in Bristol by the Herreshoff Boat Yard in 1887. Beginning in the 1950s, the Pearson Yacht Company in Bristol was one of the first boatyards to use fiberglass in boats. Fiberglass boats are cheaper and easier to produce than handmade wooden boats. Fiberglass is strong, can be molded into many forms, and is very lightweight.

Vanguard Sailboats in Portsmouth is the largest seller in North America of the Optimist Dinghy, the fiberglass sailboat many children learn to sail.

Attractions and Landmarks

Rhode Island attracts many visitors to the state. Newport, Providence, and the South County beaches are the most popular spots to visit, but there are many other places as well.

HISTORIC SITES

Located on a hillside facing the Pawtuxet River, the Nathanael Greene Homestead was built in 1770. During the **Revolutionary War** (1775–1783), Greene was second in command to George Washington.

Originally known as Spell Hall, Nathanael Greene lived here from 1770 to 1776.

The house includes two main floors, each of which has four rooms and a central hall. Each room contains a fireplace and three large windows. The home's interior was restored between 1919 and 1924, after the house was turned into a museum. The rooms are furnished with period furniture and Greene family items. In front of the house sits a cannon that was probably made at the family forge in Potowomut.

Fort Adams in Newport is the nation's largest coastal fort. The early settlers knew that Narragansett Bay was a major waterway and had to be defended. The first fort, built around 1700, was made of earth and **masonry,** surrounded by a ditch, and protected by bastions. Bastions are arrow-shaped protections along a wall that help keep the enemy away. The present fort, built between 1824 and 1857, is unique because it has narrow rooms under the ditches, underground listening galleries, and large earth-filled walls to protect it from the enemy.

Today, Fort Adams is a state park containing the Museum of Yachting, which is devoted to the history of yachting in Newport. *Courageous,* the state yacht, and other historic boats are on the grounds of the museum. The museum sponsors the Traditional Boat Building School to teach students about building and repairing wooden boats.

Fort Adams is now a popular spot for sailing in Narragansett Bay.

Trinity Church in Newport was built between 1725 and 1726, and is a unique church. It has the nation's only three-tiered center aisle pulpit. The three sections of the pulpit are a preaching desk, a reading desk, and a clerk's desk. The pulpit is also unique because it is positioned in the center of the aisle, rather than near a sidewall of the church. George Washington in 1781 and Queen Elizabeth II of Great Britain in 1976 worshipped in Pew 81.

The Cocumscussoc Archeological Site provides a look at Rhode Island history, featuring historical buildings, gardens and archeological work on the property. It is located in Wickford on land that Roger Williams established as a trading post in the 1630s. The post was destroyed during **King Philip's War** (1675-1676). In 1678, Richard Smith, a farmer, bought the property and started one of the colony's first dairy herds. The dairy farm thrived for more than three hundred years. In

Places to See in Rhode Island

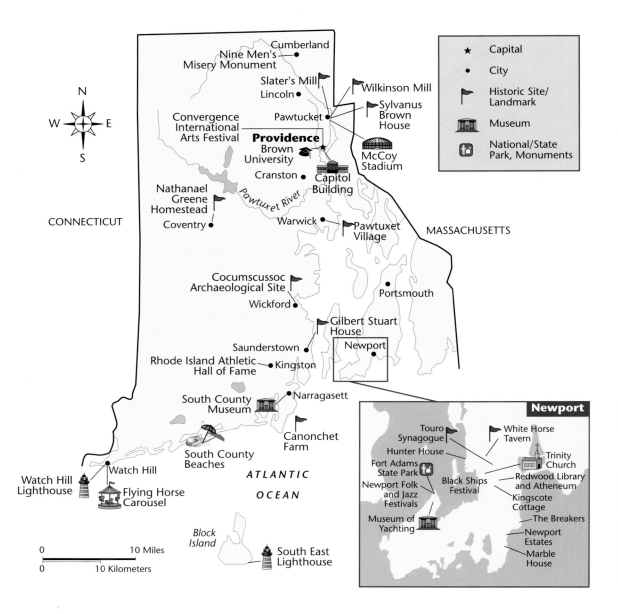

1740, Daniel Updike, the Attorney General of Rhode Island, expanded the property into a working plantation. Today, visitors to the site can see how Rhode Island's early colonists lived and worked.

Gilbert Stuart (1755–1828) was one of the nation's most famous portrait painters. His painting of George Washington was the model for the president's portrait on the one-dollar bill. Located in Saunderstown, and built in

1751, the Stuart house has been carefully restored to its 18th-century appearance. Visitors can peer into rooms with the unique corner fireplaces, furnishings from the mid-1700s, and reproductions of Stuart's portraits. The family kitchen includes a Dutch oven, a collection of household items and cooking utensils from the 1700s and a snuff mill similar to the one the Stuart's father would have used to grind tobacco into snuff. Just outside the house is a restored gristmill, similar to the one that once ground grain into flour for the area's farmers.

Gilbert Stuart painted portraits of presidents George Washington, John Adams, Thomas Jefferson, James Madison, and James Monroe.

Brown University, founded in Providence in 1764, is the third-oldest college in New England and the ninth-oldest in the United States. It was originally called Rhode Island College. In the early 1800s, the college needed to raise money. It decided that in return for a donation of $5,000, the donor would be able to name the college. A graduate, Nicholas Brown, quickly made the generous gift. In September 1804, the college's name was changed to "Brown University in Providence in the State of Rhode Island, and Providence Plantations."

GEOGRAPHIC SITES

Block Island is located twelve miles from the Rhode Island coast at the eastern entrance to Long Island Sound. On the island is the Block Island South East Lighthouse, which was built in 1875. The tower is 52 feet high and is attached to the keeper's house. Also

43

In 1993, the Block Island Southeast Lighthouse had to be moved 360 feet inland because of erosion.

on the grounds are two cisterns, which gathered runoff water used for drinking and bathing, and a boathouse.

Located in Jamestown, 153-acre Beavertail State Park is famous for some of the most beautiful seascapes along the New England coastline. Visitors come from all over the country to enjoy the park's sights and hike along the rocky coastline. The waters that lap the shore offer some of the best saltwater fishing in the area. The park is open year-round.

Map of Rhode Island

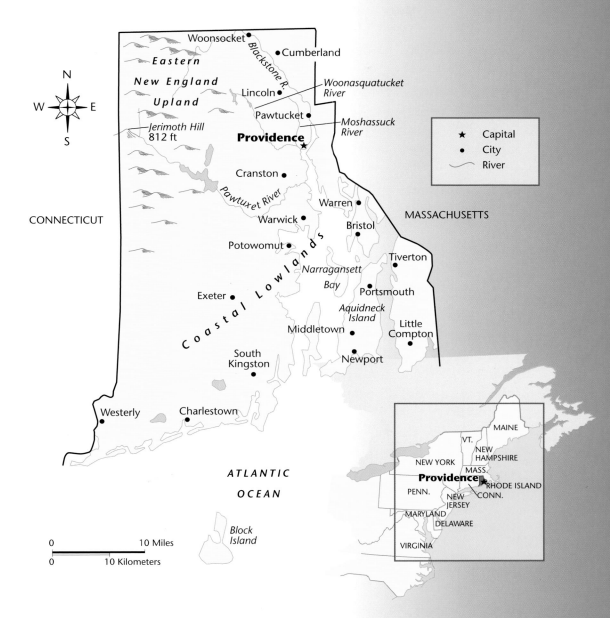

N
W — E
S

Woonsocket
Cumberland

Blackstone R.

Eastern
New England
Upland

Lincoln

Woonasquatucket River

Pawtucket

Providence ★

Moshassuck River

Jerimoth Hill 812 ft

Cranston

Pawtuxet River

Warren

Capital ★
City ●
River ∿

CONNECTICUT

Warwick

Bristol

MASSACHUSETTS

Potowomut

Narragansett Bay

Tiverton

Coastal Lowlands

Exeter

Portsmouth

Aquidneck Island

Little Compton

Middletown

South Kingston

Newport

Westerly

Charlestown

ATLANTIC OCEAN

Block Island

0   10 Miles
0   10 Kilometers

MAINE
VT.
NEW HAMPSHIRE
NEW YORK
MASS.
Providence ★ RHODE ISLAND
PENN.
NEW JERSEY CONN.
MARYLAND
DELAWARE
VIRGINIA

45

Glossary

agate a gemstone that can be polished for jewelry or other uses

America's Cup a famous yacht race

anthropologists social scientists who study the cultures of people

appeals legal cases that are sent to a higher court for review

archeological relating to the social science that studies the cultural remains of ancient people

atheneum a library

Baptist a member of a Protestant religious group

carousel a merry-go-round

charter a legal document that grant specific rights, such as self-government

circumnavigate to sail around the world

civil cases those cases that relate to the rights of individuals

Civil War (1861–1865) the war between the Union (the North) and the Confederacy (the South) fought over issues such as states' rights and slavery

conservation to work to save or preserve nature

constitution a written plan of government for a country or a state

Continental Congress the temporary government of the Thirteen Colonies while they were fighting Great Britain during the Revolutionary War

dinghies small rubber boats

discrimination unfair treatment of a group or an individual

explorers people who search for new places or information

federal government the national government

felony cases cases that involve serious crimes, which are usually punishable by a penalty of more than one year in jail in addition to fines

filigree detailed patterns in metal or jewelry

Friends' Meetinghouse a Quaker house of worship

Gothic Revival a style of architecture influenced by medieval styles, characterized by lines flowing up to a pointed arch

immigrant a person who leaves one country and settles in another one

independence freedom from control of others

Ivy League the athletic conference that includes the prominent universities of Brown, Columbia, Cornell, Dartmouth, Harvard, Penn, Princeton, and Yale

King Philip's War (1675–1676) a violent conflict between American colonists and Native Americans

legislature a group of elected people who make laws for a state or a country

masonry relating to bricks

misdemeanors less serious crimes

46

patriotic love for one's country

persecution the act of causing harm to people because of their beliefs or lifestyle

pharmaceutical relating to medicines and drugs

poultry chicken, turkey, duck, and other fowl raised for food

Quakers a religious group that opposes war

ratify to approve

Renaissance a period in history beginning in the late 1400s, when the arts and learning thrived

renovated remodeled or rebuilt

resolution a formal opinion expressed by a group, such as a council or congress

Revolutionary War (1775–1783) the war in which the thirteen American colonies won independence from Great Britain

royal charter a legal document, granted by a king or a queen, that grant specific rights, such as self-government

separation of church and state the idea that government and religion are not connected to each other

slavery a condition in which one person is the property of another

synagogue a Jewish temple or house of worship

temperate mild; not extreme

textile cloth or fabric

toleration to accept other people's differences

topiary plants that are trimmed into shapes of animals or other characters

Torah Jewish scripture

torpedo boat a small high-speed boat

veterans men and women who have served in the military

World War II (1939–1945) war in which the United States, the United Kingdom, and their allies defeated Germany, Italy, and Japan

More Books to Read

• •

Kling, Andrew. *Rhode Island.* San Diego, CA: Lucent Books, 2002.

Heinrichs, Ann. *Rhode Island.* Minneapolis, MN: Compass Point Books, 2004.

McNair, Sylvia. *Rhode Island.* New York: Children's Press, 2000.

Whitehurst, Susan. *Colony of Rhode Island.* New York: PowerKids Press, 2000.

Index

About the Authors

Katie Barney Moose has lived in both Newport and Providence and is descended from several of the original settlers of Rhode Island, including the Brown family. She is the author of six books about Rhode Island and Maryland.

D. J. Ross is a writer and educator with more than 25 years of experience in education. Ross has traveled throughout the United States, and now lives in the Midwest with three basset hounds.